**W9-ALL-999**

G7

WELCOME TO THE WORLD OF ANIMALS

Wild Cats

Diane Swanson

Gareth Stevens Publishing
MILWAUKEE

For a free color catalog describing Gareth Stevens' list of high-quality books and multimedia programs, call 1-800-542-2595 (USA) or 1-800-461-9120 (Canada).
Gareth Stevens Publishing's Fax: (414) 225-0377.
See our catalog, too, on the World Wide Web: http://gsinc.com

The publishers acknowledge the support of the Canada Council for the Arts and the Cultural Services Branch of the Government of British Columbia in making this publication possible.

Library of Congress Cataloging-in-Publication Data

Swanson, Diane, 1944-
    [Welcome to the world of wild cats]
    Wild cats / by Diane Swanson.
        p. cm. — (Welcome to the world of animals)
    Originally published: Welcome to the world of wild cats. North Vancouver, B.C.:
Whitecap Books, © 1997.
    Includes index.
    Summary: Describes the physical characteristics and behavior of such
North American wild cats as the lynx, bobcat, and mountain lion.
    ISBN 0-8368-2217-X (lib. bdg.)
    1. Felidae—Juvenile literature. [1. Felidae. 2. Cats.] I. Title. II. Series:
Swanson, Diane, 1944-   Welcome to the world of animals.
QL737.C23S88   1998
599.75—dc21   98-6599

This North American edition first published in 1998 by
Gareth Stevens Publishing
1555 North RiverCenter Drive, Suite 201
Milwaukee, WI 53212 USA

This U.S. edition © 1998 by Gareth Stevens, Inc. Original edition © 1997 by Diane Swanson.
First published in 1997 by Whitecap Books, Vancouver/Toronto.
Additional end matter © 1998 by Gareth Stevens.

Gareth Stevens series editor: Dorothy L. Gibbs
Editorial assistant: Diane Laska
Cover design: Renee M. Bach

Cover photograph: Thomas Kitchin/First Light
Photo credits: Chase Swift/First Light 4; Thomas Kitchin/First Light 6, 8, 10, 14, 18, 20, 24, 26, 30;
Victoria Hurst/First Light 12, 16, 22; Daniel J. Cox/First Light 28.

Printed in Mexico

1 2 3 4 5 6 7 8 9 02 01 00 99 98

Contents

World of Difference

Sleek wild cats slip silently through the night. Walking on their toes, with their claws held in, they move nimbly, even across narrow ledges. When they spring, strong back legs push them into high leaps. When they jump down, they swivel their bodies to land lightly on their feet.

There are about three dozen kinds of wild cats around the world, including lions, tigers, leopards — and more. In North America, there are three main cats: bobcats, lynx, and mountain lions. People call a mountain lion by many different names,

This mountain lion is on the alert, watching for signs of prey and danger.

5

The lynx has snowshoe feet. It runs quickly and easily across winter's blanket of snow.

such as cougar, puma, panther, deer tiger, painter, and catamount.

The mountain lion is the biggest wild cat in both the United States and Canada. It can stand as tall as a kitchen table and weigh more than 220 pounds (100 kilograms) — about ten times the weight of an average bobcat or a small lynx.

The mountain lion's coat is spotted as a kitten and grows plain-colored as an adult. Except for black trim on its face and tail tip, its coat is usually gray or reddish brown.

Most bobcats have coats with spots or bars on them. Even their short tails are marked with a black bar.

Lynx have longer, thicker fur that is often yellow-brown and spotted. Short, black fur tips their stubby tails, and tall, black fur tips their ears.

GONE WILD

A long time ago, all cats were wild. Gradually, some kinds were tamed and became pets that lived with people. Sometimes pet cats that are left alone can turn wild again. They hunt for their food and raise their kittens the same way mountain lions, lynx, and bobcats do.

These wild "pets" are called feral cats. They live in cities — in parks, sewers, and warehouses. The males usually live alone. The females often live in groups and raise their kittens together.

Where in the World

Forests, swamps, and grasslands are some of the different areas wild cats claim as homes, or territories. Mountain lions usually look for rough, rocky places that could be high on mountain slopes or down at sea level.

Some mountain lions and bobcats choose dry, desertlike areas. Others live in soggy swamplands. Bobcats and lynx are strong swimmers. Mountain lions can swim, too, but they would rather jump across water. They can easily leap more than 13 feet (4 meters).

This bobcat blends with the colors of its rocky home.

9

Whenever it can, the mountain lion leaps over water to avoid swimming.

Many mountain lions, lynx, and bobcats live in or around forests. Lynx prefer thick woods for resting and raising their families, but, for hunting, they like land with more bushes and fewer trees.

The size of a wild cat's territory changes. If there is plenty of food around, cats claim small territories. If prey is scarce, their territories can be huge. Cats mark the borders of their territories with their smell. A mountain lion, for example, scrapes up piles of dirt or leaves around its territory and adds its scent to them.

There are fewer wild cats today than there used to be. Mountain lions can be found in South America and western North America; lynx in Alaska, Canada, northern Europe and Asia, and the northern United States; and bobcats from southern Canada to Mexico.

TIGERS OF TIMES PAST

A saber-toothed tiger — bigger than a mountain lion — slips through tall grass, hunting for prey. It creeps close to a mammoth elephant, then leaps. Grasping its prey tightly, the tiger drives two huge fangs deep into the mammoth's throat.

This scene might have taken place long ago. Saber-toothed tigers do not hunt anymore. Like mammoths, they have disappeared. In all of North America, South America, and Europe, only their bones remain today.

11

World of the Hunter

As hunters, cats are masters. They are built for catching prey. Their perky ears pick up sounds as soft as the scampering of a squirrel and as high as the squeak of a mouse. Their big eyes let in lots of light to help them see in darkness. Their movable whiskers sense anything close — even without touching it.

Surprise works well for these hunters. They pounce on prey and grab it with razor-sharp claws. Then, using their whiskers and long teeth, they feel for the best place to bite — usually in the neck.

This bobcat has settled down to eat its catch — a ring-necked pheasant.

One bite is often all a wild cat needs.

When a wild cat feeds, its rough tongue scrapes the meat off the bones, and the grooved roof of its mouth helps grind up skin and bones.

In North America, all wild cats catch small prey, such as mice, rabbits, and birds. A lynx

Mmm, porcupine! This mountain lion is going after lunch. It also hunts big prey, such as elk and bighorn sheep.

likes to eat snowshoe hares, which are rabbitlike animals with long back legs and large feet. The more snowshoe hares there are in an area, the more lynx move in to hunt them.

Although a lynx or a bobcat might hunt a deer for food, a deer is usually prey for a mountain lion. As big as this cat is, it might take two or three weeks to eat a whole deer. Sometimes the cat will drag the deer nearly $^1/4$ mile ($^1/2$ kilometer) to find a good hiding place for it until the next meal.

PICK A PRICKLY PORCUPINE

A porcupine for dinner probably would not be your choice, but it might be a mountain lion's pick. The cat will toss the creature — and all 30,000 quills — onto its back and start eating the animal from its bare underside.

What about those sharp quills? The mountain lion chews — and digests — some of them. A few might stick in its paws and face, but most fall out later. Quills that work their way under the cat's skin usually dissolve over time.

World of Words

Living alone, cats are not big talkers. When they must talk, however, they say a lot. They use sounds, signs, and actions to scare enemies and attract mates.

If people, wolves, or threatening cats come near, a wild cat might lean forward, twist its ears backward, bare its teeth, and hiss-s-s-s. Even a kitten hisses loudly at an enemy. A grown cat sometimes growls low and spits, too — just another way to say, "Get lost."

When they talk, smaller cats, such as bobcats and lynx, might try to make

"I'm worried," this mountain lion is saying. When mountain lions are scared, they usually leap into trees.

17

The lynx growls low and stares hard at another lynx, hoping to scare it away.

themselves look bigger and tougher by standing tall and raising their ears. Bobcats sometimes threaten by twisting their ears and showing the white spots on the backs of them.

An enemy cat might respond by flattening its ears and lowering its tail.

18

Then, it might slowly sneak away as if to say, "You win."

When wild cats look for mates, they mark soil, bushes, and trees with scents from their saliva, urine, and body oils. Its scent identifies each cat and announces that it is ready to mate. The cat might also scratch the ground or the trees around its territory.

Wild cats speak to their mates, too. Females make piercing screams to send long-distance messages to males. Close to their mates, wild cats meow and gurgle like bubbling water to say, "I'm friendly."

A PUR-R-R-FECT FEELING

"Pur-r-r-r, pur-r-r-r," says a wild kitten snuggling close to its mother. It purrs as it drinks warm milk from its mother's body. It purrs as it breathes in and out. Purring is how a kitten says, "I'm feeling pur-r-r-fectly fine."

The wild cat mother purrs, too. The steady sound soothes her kittens. Purring is how she tells them, "All is well." Not only is it comforting, but it is a safe way to talk. Purrs are too soft for the cat's enemies to hear.

19

New World

Spring brings many wild kittens, but baby bobcats and mountain lions can be born at any time of the year.

Wild cat mothers give birth to two or more small kittens in cozy dens — sheltered spots inside caves, under rock piles, beneath tree roots, or among thick bushes. Even the largest — the mountain lion kitten — weighs no more than what three or four bananas might weigh.

Newborns are helpless and need a lot of care. They cannot even open their eyes for over a week. Their mother snuggles them

A bobcat kitten feels safe near its mother. Like other wild cats, it might live about fifteen years.

21

This four-week-old lynx kitten waits in some thick bushes for its mother to return.

to keep them warm and licks them to keep them clean. She feeds them with her milk for hours at a time.

Soon, however, the mother cat must hunt to feed herself. The kittens stay in the den. By this time, they can crawl a little, so they nestle together to warm up or wriggle apart to cool down. Their mother does not go far, and she returns often to check on them.

A wild cat mother has to change dens sometimes to keep her family safe. She carries each kitten to the new den by gently grabbing loose skin at the back of its neck with her mouth.

Wild kittens feed on their mother's milk for two months or more. Gradually, she adds meat to their meals until they no longer need her milk. Then she teaches the kittens how to catch their own food.

NO SITTER NEEDED

A hungry mother bobcat creeps out of her cave. There is no one to watch her sleeping kittens, but no one is needed. Boulders hide the cave well. The cat has left her kittens there many nights before. In fact, this family is the third one she has trusted to this den.

While she is gone, the kittens wake up. They are hungry, but they do not make a sound. Side by side, they wait by the entrance to the den, watching and listening for mom's return.

Small World

Rough tongues make good combs. Wild cat mothers use them to pull loose hairs and dirt from their kittens' soft coats. Grooming her kittens is just one of a mother cat's duties. The biggest job is teaching them how — and what — to hunt.

Lessons begin when a mother brings her prey to the den. At first, the kittens just watch her eat. Later, they start playing with the prey, and, soon, they are nibbling at it. One day, the mother brings her kittens some prey that is only stunned or wounded. Then they practice pouncing.

Grooming two five-month-old kittens keeps this mountain lion mother busy.

Before long, the kittens are ready to go hunting with their mother. They watch as she creeps close to her prey and leaps on it. Then they try to do the same.

All the while, the mother cat watches. Coyotes and other predators, such as eagles and big owls, might try to take her

Following a mountain lion mom in winter sometimes means getting a face full of snow.

young. If she senses danger, she growls. The kittens stand as still as statues while she checks for trouble.

Wild kittens hunt with their mothers until they can hunt for themselves. For bobcats and lynx, that might be only a year, but mountain lions stay with their mothers up to twenty months. Because they hunt large prey, they need more time to practice their skills.

When it is time, wild cat mothers shoo their kittens away. Their small, safe world suddenly grows big.

COOL CATS

On hot days, wild cats know how to keep cool. They pant, and they sweat — mostly through the pads of their feet. They nap in the shade, stretching out to let their body heat escape. Sometimes they even lie down in water.

Cats also keep a cool head. Blood that travels through the skin in their noses loses heat, then flows to the base of the brain. This cooler blood picks up and carries away heat from blood that enters the brain.

Fun World

Any time is a good time for cat play. In one popular game, a kitten flops down, tummy up. Its back legs start "cycling," and its front legs slap the air. A second kitten leaps beside the first one and paws at it furiously. Then — flip, flip — the kittens trade places, and the game starts again.

Wild kittens often play alone. They leap at bushes, chase moths, and attack rolling leaves. They play with prey, batting at it and tossing it around. Games like these help cats learn to judge distance and know when to strike. Playing gives them

Run! Pounce! Young mountain lions play fast games that build good hunting skills.

a chance to practice their hunting skills.

Playing also gives kittens exercise that helps them grow healthy and strong. It teaches them to listen carefully, watch closely, and react quickly when there is danger.

Wild cats play at all ages. Some adults play with each

A tiny bobcat practices tree-climbing by playing.

other before they mate. Mother cats play with their kittens, wrestling, boxing, and grabbing at their heads. In these gentle scuffles, one furry body wraps around another and another. Now and then, the kittens break free. Then they leap over their mother, pretending to escape.

Like human children, kittens play more than adults. They play hard until they get tired. When one kitten has finally had enough, it might jump into the air to signal the end of the game. Enough fun — for now.

WILD CAT WONDERS

Wild cats are wildly wonderful. Here are some reasons why:

- **The daggerlike teeth of ancient saber-toothed tigers were as long as the blade of a bread knife.**

- **When their whiskers brush against something, cats blink to help protect their eyes.**

- **Cats see well in only one-sixth the light people need.**

- **Over twenty muscles swivel a cat's ear toward a soft sound.**

Glossary

den — a sheltered place, such as a cave, where a wild animal lives or hides from danger.

feral — living wild after being tame, such as a pet that has run away.

groom — to make something look clean and neat.

pads — the soft cushions on the bottoms of the feet of some animals, such as cats and dogs.

pant — (v) to breathe in short, quick puffs, or gasps, sometimes as a way to cool off.

scampering — running or moving quickly from place to place, usually in a playful way.

scuffle — (n) a tangled, mixed-up fight or struggle that usually does not last very long.

soggy — very wet; soaked with water.

stunned — not able to think or act normally, sometimes because of an attack.

territory — the area where an animal or a group of animals finds food and makes its home.

Index